M000033967

i am not a princess, i am a complete fairytale

written by nivedita lakhera
edited by shefali bhakuni

illustrations by nivedita lakhera
photographs by stephanie masullo

special thanks to all these courageous, inspiring women
for sharing their valued and sensitive life stories, helping
infuse hope and bravery in the lives of countless women
across the world

copyright © 2019 by nivedita lakhera

all rights reserved. no part of this book may be used
or reproduced in any manner whatsoever without
written permission

except
in case of reprints in the context of reviews.

published in united states of america,
first printing, 2019
isbn-10: 0998434981
isbn-13: 978-0998434988

attention: schools, universities, libraries and businesses
the book is available at quantity discounts with bulk
purchase for education, business or sales promotional use.
for information please contact at website-
niveditalakhera.com

there is nothing heavier than unsaid words
set them free, set them free

you must begin with the truth,
that's where your roots will birth your full story

my hair is super wavy- rebellious like my soul- and for the
last decade, i have been flat ironing it to the point of exhaustion.

writing the book *i am not a princess i am a complete fairytale* was
an emotional ride, i cried reading the testaments of some of
the women mentioned here and felt a sense of pride and honor
that now they are a part of me. i felt vulnerable throwing myself
bare on its pages and holding my breath; i remember needing to
take a walk after writing one poem because it was just that
overpowering. but writing this book made me brave, brave enough
to now enjoy my curls- my waves- my oceanic pride.

i have alopecia areata, pcos, a history of stroke, physical trauma,
and a stent inserted inside my left middle cerebral artery to keep
the blood flowing in a vital part of my brain.

i used to fight all of this, but with this book, i have accepted all of
me-half broken, half-healed, a quarter of a person may be at times,
but full-hearted, fully alive, and fully embracing all of me- caressing
my soul when i fall down, on those days when my right leg feels weak
and my right hand too fatigued to work. i sing to them and thank
them from my heart for doing the best they can. with maybe half a
brain but complete courage, i can tell you, there is always a reason
to find joy and fulfillment, there is always the option to be brave,
and i hope you choose it, because courage is the foundation of
authentic life, courage allows you to pursue life of your dreams,
courage allows you to be you.

you are alive, let's make a life out of this living, so share your
stories in *nivedita lakhera fan page* on facebook, your story
may inspire someone who is about to give up.

your story may save a life. such is the power of words.

and remember to sing loud to yourself, every now and then,
i am not a princess i am a complete fairytale.
love you all, let us begin our journey into the world of words.

the death before the birth

it made her homeless
when there was nothing
safe anymore
not even her body,
not even her soul

when he took her body
in bits, in pieces
she became part skin
part flesh, part pain

and a whole lot less

she had to separate herself
from herself to rise above
the unsafe land into the sky

and witness the theft of herself in real time

she had to separate herself
from herself
and expand into otherness
to hug tight to infuse
her soul back into that
broken, beaten, bitten body

how does a six-year-old do that?
because
she does not know how to die ye

...

she only knows
that she has to go home and
protect her family because he said
if you say anything, i will kill them all

her small brain, her big heart- kept her up at night,
carrying fear and pain- bigger than her inside
she never learnt how to sleep
   ...

one day i will be taller than all of this
she decided
one day i will be the biggest warrior
to protect those who cannot protect themselves

and she started building herself
wherever she was
however she was, from whatever she had

and she read, and she read
the imagination became her parents
fairytales became the safe life
stories became the soldiers
knowledge became the power
and books became the fort

and words

words covered her
bleeding, exposed, wounds on her soul

we won't let you scar
we won't let you scar
we will make sure you heal back to softness

and they kept their promises
and they kept their promises

dedicated to gomti mehata

"i grew up in a slum in delhi, my father was a daily wage
laborer and my mother worked in a factory where she
sorted plastic collected from garbage. i have two brothers
and a sister. my dad always told all of us, if we want to get
out of the slum, we need education.

those words were the key to my motivation. i couldn't wait
to go to school, waited everyday outside of the school
till i turn five years old. i studied all the time. i started
working when i was ten years old so i could get stationery
and books for school.

a lot of bad things happened, one being getting raped at
the age of 13 but a lot of good things happened too,
such as meeting the angel when i finished my diploma,
who turned my life around, gave me shelter, love, education,
a normal life which i missed throughout my childhood.

don't let people define you or your life,
don't let anyone tell you what you can or should do
and you can't and shouldn't do."

gomti mehata

you are
none of the things
that happened to you

you are everything what you did
with all those experiences

there is no place, there is no place
i repeat,
there is no place,

you cannot come back from

till you are breathing
one foot after another
keep going keep going

there is no place you cannot come back from

i set me on fire
to burn down

all that was not me

distillation of self

faith that will save us all

we must believe in good
even when we are in the middle of
everything not so good
or in extreme bad situation,

we cannot let hate to consume us, distract us

we must believe in the good and love
because that's the only way forward-
not only for saving of our souls,
but also, for our future generations

we must keep doing what is right –
when we are wronged left and right,
especially when we are wronged left and right

we must keep choosing love-
even when we are hated by every corner,
especially when we have only been receiving hatred

no other time in our life-
love will have greater importance
than the times we are tempted not to choose it
so be tenacious-
that's the only religion that the universe needs from you
and that needs the highest form of bravery

that's the only way forward
and to those spreading hate,
we will keep sending you baskets full of love
till you get tired of hatred and see how useless it is
we will keep setting example
why love is all we need-in the middle of hatred,
the only way to end animosity is by creating kinship

just because you are broken
doesn't mean you are not wholesome

all the pieces that are you, are glorious,
whether together or apart

one day,

you won't just get
taller than your pain,

but you will realize
you climbed over it

and it took you to the land
you actually belonged to,
you always belonged to

let your soul grow taller

your past, your present, your future
is not the most beautiful thing about you,

'you' are

the timeless glory that you are

the grace of acceptance

you can love yourself and still let go of the old you
when that doesn't serve the purpose of
why you are in this world

a butterfly can't hold onto its shell of pupa
after it has the knowledge of its wings,
she can't crawl now

she needs to accept wings, sky, garden, flowers
she needs to celebrate new reasons and new seasons
its purpose is to reach flowers, add beauty and do its dance

you can love yourself without the condition of permanence
- you can fall in love with the change that you are-
you can become a process

that's the beginning of learning to love
without attachment
it starts first with you and your love with who you are
and replacing it with who you can be, need to be,
deserve to be

you can love yourself enough to bury the old you
and grow a new you
that's the beginning of learning to love
without attachment

that's the first death that you can learn
to understand and accept

all the phases of the moon are lovely, needed, and beautiful

you have ended several years from now,
now do you feel free to begin
something beautiful and something

new

each ending has the capacity and audacity
for new beginnings- allow that birth

healing is not linear

healing is not linear,
grief is not linear

there are days where victory songs come
rainbows carry all the same bright colors
and then some more
and your chest feels light enough to breathe again

till a memory walks on it with feet carrying
mountains that may not even belong to this land
such foreign weight which
no tongue has ever known to speak of

you want to go back to the days
where this pain did not exist
there was no intention of it,
the joy that was as stubborn as light in the sun

but the new days
and all the days following
won't have the same hours, seconds of radiance
but a few will have absence of light
and a few will have claws of despair

and that's when you say it out loud
healing is not linear, grief is not linear
healing is not linear, grief is not linear

once you make peace with this fact
the jagged margins of journey don't bleed
but become friends
where you can spend hours talking about
how uninteresting smooth roads are...

and how much you needed
to see other paths
even those with less glitter,

rich with absence of light at times,
shade to rest-
before you begin again and again

and that's what acceptance looks like

and you sink in the comfort of knowing
that no, you don't have to make sense
of all of this right now

but you do need to do
a little something good for you today
or a lot of good for you today
even when nothing feels good,
especially when nothing feels good

and you do need to do
a little something good for someone else today
or a lot of good for someone else today
even when nothing feels good,
especially when nothing feels good

and you need to keep going
till roads get tired of your feet

not the other way around,
not the other way around

dedicated to dr renee mathur and dr leslie wilson

"this is one of the poems i read at my father's funeral.
this poem means a lot to me.
everyday i remind me that grief is not linear.
it gives me permission to have moments of sadness and
not feel guilty about moments of joy."

 dr leslie wilson

"grief is not linear. i write this on sympathy cards, because
it is true and needs to be heard. no one told me this, but
until you experience great loss, you think grief and healing
are linear. they are not. I was born quite late in the lives of
my parents. a surprise, shock, 'gift from god.' i grew up as an
only child in my house as my brothers were 16 and 20 years
older, and on with their lives. as i was the only little one in
my extended family, i was given much attention. and my mother
treated me as the greatest gift she'd ever been given. spoiled
rotten. but what a bond.
i realized my mom was older, and i was terrified of losing her
in my youth. but dear Irene lived to 82, and died suddenly,
without much suffering or prolonged illness.
sudden death of an older parent is merciful. no pain.
no suffering. but, oh, so, sudden. i immediately felt huge sorrow,
gratitude, more sorrow, and more gratitude. then the acute,
overwhelming period of mourning passed. i forged on.
and i expected the recovery to be a straight path.
a diagonal line on a graph. every day better, missing her less,
hurting less. no. i would be in a store, and see a piece of some
clothing she'd like and start to buy it. but she was gone. i'd see
a funny bit on tv and laugh her same giggly laugh (she had such
a great silly, snarky wit) and think to call her. no. like walking
on a flat paved street and falling into a manhole. suddenly
falling straight down.

grief is not linear."

dr renee mathur

learning awareness is knowledge
practicing awareness is wisdom
becoming awareness is transcendence

shame, but why

once upon a time it was decided
honor was the responsibility of women

shame was manufactured
so they could be enslaved

virginity became their responsibility
character got tied with their sexuality
the onus of keeping together the family
was also given to them

so was vanity invented,
and songs, movies, ads, magazines,
movies were manufactured
how a beautiful woman
should look like
and what beauty should be

a complete woman, lady-like,
family woman, such terms were coined
to aim for validation of their existence
having it all and what not

so, the hamster in the wheel
never got a chance to do anything
but run and then die, never were they allowed
to pause and ask simple questions

...

like, why periods should be embarrassing
despite being the sign of sustaining life on planet earth,
a thing that should be celebrated
a sign of fertility became a shameful thing

...

why her sexuality became a taboo
and woman had to be a goddess,
and sacredness tied to that, not in her selflessness
to serve people in her lives, friends, society,
kindness, integrity, but to her sexuality

why her honor was stitched to her vagina,
someone else assaults her private parts
but she should hang her head in shame
as if her entire existence now has no meaning
and she should either die or marry the culprit

why is a single woman half a woman
why is a childless woman assumed empty of life

i am getting off that wheel i am no hamster
and i am more than what they tell me i should be

my pain my healing my journey
and i will make sure i write
my own story with the ink of courage
i will walk on fire but it will be my path
not your hamster wheels
with that i say #me too,

let the healing begin

claiming my soul

shame is one of the most manipulative social norms being used
to control any subset of population, shame is the artificial fear
created by few in society against your truth, that it's not ready
for you or your truth,
just remember it is not your cross to bear,
it's their fear, compulsive need to control you-
just remember it's their problem, their shame and their fear,

you may not belong to any constellation,
but you decorate and mark 'north'

and every universe needs a north star
you do not need to always belong to be required

just because you are not like somebody
doesn't mean you are nobody

unique you, is, uniquely you

you should write your story
it's a rare freedom
and only a few have it

you must respect and honor that

for when you write it,
you will be its greatest audience

your jaw will drop for
how far you have come

and what breathlessly unique art
you have created
with all that you had
and all that you went in search for

so, you should write your story

illustrate your journey, it carries inspiration for many

it's not the path,
you were taught to take,

it's the path,
you were born to take

unlearn

and one day you will become
whatever you work towards becoming

you are what you do, walk towards you

melanin that had to sell its pride

she rubbed soap

and bleach and creams
and whatnot
and brush against
her every inch

so her gorgeous
rich cinnamon skin
to turn into
pristine moon color

the way
it's on every 'pretty girl'

'because that's what 'pretty' is

but how can she reach that how

she can't work hard on that
she can't jump to the sky
and rub moon-dust
all over her, she can only buy
what they are selling on the screen

...

she sets fire to her curls
how do i straighten my tresses
she burns the beautiful hair
passed as gifts from
her great grandmother to her grandmother

then she marks her body
where islands and rivers curved
the way they are supposed to
in those distant alive exotic lands

but it was foreign and tribal
as per 'them',
not the way it's supposed to be

she bleeds and jumps
and cuts till her body matches
all the pages in vogue

last, she untwists
her thick tongue rich with sounds
with blessings of ancestors

seasoned with voices of friends,
songs, streets, spices
old addresses, teachers
and neighbors, seasons and plants

...

she washes herself with shame
showered by frowns
of those 'better people'
she irons the waves of her oceanic voice
into a correct accent

till she gets to
the mirror

she knows not the person she sees, but is relieved
that she will now belong to the land of opportunity
and will walk with no objection

dedicated to vanessa rochelle lewis

'the first day that i walked into my predominantly black,
christian preschool class (there was one white boy with red hair,
freckles, and so much personality), a little boy looked at me
and immediately screamed something along the lines of,
 "oh my god, why you look like that?"

"like what," i asked, genuinely curious.
"ugly," another boy said, opening the doors to giggles, chuckles,
and shouts of agreement.

"you look burnt, black, and fat," the original boy said,
laughing even harder. pretty soon the class was a writhing,
joyful hoot of solidarity and my unappealing appearance
was the unifying factor.

it took me till a little after thirty to stop searching for solace
and validation, running from the impact, and hiding from
other people and myself. to stay alive. to truly accept, in my
heart, that beauty, ugly, and everything in between is a lie
that serves a purpose. that purpose is oppression, is supremacy,
is control and is money.

understanding that keeps me from internalizing the pain
and believing the myths of universal beauty standards,
objective ugliness, or that any of that should inform
how i think about me and others.
understanding that heals the very real psychological,
social, and systemic impact of being perceived as one of the
ugly people, and keeps me free enough to recognize my magic,
to share that magic with others, and to celebrate the magic
that is shared with me. "

vanessa rochelle lewis

i am not going to cut myself into half
because you have not learnt to love someone whole

your desire of me
dwarfs in front of my desire to be complete

say no to those who try to trim your fire,
forgetting you are a sun,

do not become less for no one

you matter

black lives matter, black deaths matter

they demand
my skin be lighter
so their kids
feel safe around me

they want
no hooded t shirt
on my scalding head in the heat of the day so
they feel safe around me

they have allowed
my rise in songs
and olympics and the tennis court
with their hesitation,
bowing to my god like voice and body

but they give me
the lowest ceilings
and keep me on leash
to stay under other fields

they keep their white collars
and create a small token
of my race here and there
for wall carpet of diversity

...

they want
my pain to be
mellow and scream
to be soft

they want
so much
editing of
me
they want to
take so much out of me

because
they could
not empty the hands
of my ancestors enough

they want blood
out of their bloodline too

dedicated to Trayvon Benjamin Martin

(February 5, 1995 – February 26, 2012)

start with fear
start with doubt
start with shaking hands
start with numbing pain

start with chilling wounds
start with dimming suns
start with a bleeding back
start with a still raw ache

start with all that you have
start with what all is left
start with an empty chest
start with blinding glare

start with fog
start with night
start with dawn
start with a quarter sight

start with trembling bones
start with a fractured height
start with broken dreams
start with starving for what is right

but my dear fierce warrior start you must

keep on,

wherever you are- however you are
feed your heart, stay with your soul, replenish your body
stretch your mind, prepare for an adventure
rest & repair & recover when you need to, but start you must

shine brightly
you don't owe
a darn thing to darkness
flaunt your light
celebrate your radiance
enhance your brilliance
even if it blinds them,
especially if it blinds them

no apology for your glory

and when they hush your voice,
you keep your throat in a soft safe place
and then you scream through your actions
your dance, your dreams, your art, your poetry, your love,
your heavy mind creating brilliant celestial creations

the soul that roars
through them
can never be silenced

and will eventually become
an immortal prayer of all the mortals

we are learning how not to love,
how to live without each other
to mock softness, to belittle desire, to belong,
how to make others stop loving us

run away from connections that feel cosmic
for fears that are earthly

love is oxygen
and we are wondering
why our souls are turning blue and dead

what hurt you was not love
- it was greed and fear,

choose love, choose love, choose love

dear princess
they asked, how old you are

as young as a newborn star
and as old as time itself

somewhere half-broken, half- made
and as unique as a process itself

the birth that keeps giving birth

serena

you will have to work
a hundred times harder
prove your worth
a thousand times more

still they would ask you
to be submissive
and soften your roar
but you still pounce and bounce
and attack like the lion that you are

they will worship you
and they will in a heartbeat
demean you as an outcast

you will never get a pass
you will never get a pass

still know there is a tribe
that is forming in your shadow
that is nourishing from your strength

still know that you have conquered
where people were crumbled

you will be given measures
and an acceptable tone for your protest

in a moment,
the temple that you occupied
will be stomped on by the same people
who built it

...

but you stay, you stay, you stay
and be stronger

because we need
to teach our daughters
they too can take a stand
and scream when betrayed repeatedly
as they continue to confirm their power,

your brilliance may blind them,
your rise to the sky may scare them

but you shine
like a billion suns
and unfold like the lightning
that you are

your power intimidates them
your height dwarfs their existence,
they will fail to shorten you by words
they will fail to shorten you with pitiful attempts

your legacy will remain taller than any of this
traversing from the seven skies to beyond

your legacy will remain taller
your legacy will remain taller

dedicated to serena williams

when they give up on you, it will hurt
when you give up on yourself, you will halt,

but trust me
you are gonna need you someday very very soon

never give up on yourself

even when they tell you
you can't,

you leave those words
where they came from,
and walk towards
the glory that you are

life at times will bring you
to where there is no path forward,

and you are supposed to make a new path
for a lost soul behind you,

that's the purpose of your life
to bring another soul
closer to their purpose,
and so forth and so on

so, you start where you are
with what you have
but you must start,
and you must persist
you must pursue

and above all
you must keep believing

movement that is life

so, when you don't remember
how to walk, learn to dance

*at times the heart can teach
what the mind can not*

dreams without actions make
the saddest cemeteries of the purpose that is life

unleash your passion

consent is the law

it's not an invitation till i invite you

it's not an invitation
even if we sleep in the same bed
married to each other,
legally and religiously declared man and wife

it's not an invitation
even if my dress is not
what your family, your own mind,
your strict manuals of code of conduct,
your religion, your country
or anyone, anything other than me
has decided 'appropriate'

and makes you believe
i am 'asking for it'

it's not an invitation
if i just underwent or ever undergo
gender reassignment surgery,

or if i am gender neutral,
gender fluid, gender unclear, man or woman,
labeled or not labeled,
of whatever body type,
with or without society-approved
perfections or imperfections, with or without curves

...

it's not an invitation
if i am being sensuous, demure, docile,
virgin, non-virgin, straight,
gay, bisexual, unclear,
monogamous, polyamorous, dominant,
forward, backward, as per your own interpretation

it's not an invitation
if i am homeless or a pole dancer,
stripper, rocket scientist, journalist, friend,
sex worker, doctor, drug addict,
cofounder of a company pitching you an idea,
student, struggling or established actress,
wife, daughter, sister, caretaker,
or in any and every role

it's not an invitation
if i said yes at first and then changed my mind
or if we had it one time already
so i should be ok when you feel like it again

it's not an invitation
because i got drunk, or i got sober,
or i am playing easy or hard to get
or because i am celebrating
or suppressing my sexuality or lack of it

it's not an invitation
whether i am wearing a bikini, hijab,
sari, skirt, anything whatsoever or nothing

...

it's not an invitation
it's not an invitation
it's not an invitation

till i say it is

till then you are not welcome,
and you are in violation
to the highest degree
and you are committing a crime

and it will never be my shame,
it will be your shame

oh, and while we are at it
there is no such thing
called 'asking for it'
if i want i will 'ask'

your entitlement
is not my responsibility
your ignorance will be your suffering,
not mine

just remember
it's not an invitation
till i invite you,
till i say yes,
it's a no

and as someone wise once said very well,

'no' is a complete sentence

dedicated to dr martina nicholson

"i was in the peace corps, in 1974, and i was assaulted
at gunpoint, on a rainy night by a bus driver,
when i was the only passenger left on a bus coming
back from a small village distant from our county seat,
where i had been teaching all day about water and sanitation
and public health.
he locked all the windows and the doors of the bus.
he tried to get my pants off.

luckily, i was not in a dress.
i told him to go ahead and shoot me,
but he was too full of lust to do it.

he started getting at me, and i was so terrified
i defecated. this stopped him.
it was like there was no mind left in him,
as i kept trying to reach for his sanity.
suddenly he woke up from being a mindless predator.

he let me off the bus, and i walked back
to the nearest farmhouse, covered in stool.
they were so kind, and the farm wife helped clean me up.
there was no running water, so that was a big deal.
i shook all night, and she stayed with me.

the authorities tried to humiliate me that
i was still a virgin at 24 years old.
they tried to discredit me.
in the ensuing weeks, the peace corps
used my case to try to get a law in the books against rape.
it did not happen fast, but ultimately,
several years afterward, there was a law and
i became a doctor
to help and protect those most vulnerable."

dr martina nicholson

don't rush
to pick all your pieces

walk slowly
pick them gently,
greet them kindly,
get to know them
lovingly

they are fragile
till they are together

think through,
it's a second chance
in becoming greater than before, better than before

take your time, the new you is worth it,
you my love- you are worth it

allow yourself - pace and space

if you remained authentic
irrespective of your environment,
you have been successful as a human
because the greatest freedom
of living and loving comes from that

to be authentic is to be free

i am not a certain shape or size
i am a soul manifesting through a beautiful vessel
uniquely designed for the purpose of
unfolding a wish of the universe

and so are you, it's that simple

*you are more than what meets the eye,
    you extend beyond limitation of senses*

be that person
who builds you
up no matter
what

be your friend

depression kills

you don't see the walls that trap me
that are thick, heavy, dark and so close to my skin

that my chest feels their weight every time it rises
you don't see the sadness that my smile hides

...

my success, which i created so i can hide
in the most acceptable ways,
in the least threatening ways

materials and relationships
that make me charming without fulfillment,
that make my surface glittery-
the opposite of my inside where
the absence of light has become the norm

you don't see as words and knowledge
bounce back from my frozen state

i can't seem to translate the quotes you send me
into wisdom of my actions

you don't see because your fatigue
stops you from spending yourself
towards the length of my life and easing my pain

you don't see the chains that my past has laid on me
with the hardest metals and the deepest cold

you don't see me trapped,
because every time i laughed,
it looked like freedom
every person standing next to me
looked like someone who cared
every love note looked like the truth

...

how tiring it gets how exhausted i am
to put one foot after another
while no one sees me even when they look at me

remind me why this world should deserve
another day of my existence

remind me, remind me, remind me

before it's too late that i need to put myself
before my past that i can't change

remind me that the greatest love
comes from the belly of forgiveness
and that's the only one that can set me free

and stay longer, longer than you thought will be needed
so slowly i can become one of those reminders myself

dedicated to Karen, Suzie, Kelly, Kate, Robin,
Carol and several others who we lost to depression

"it was the second semester of medical school.
i was feeling more and more frustrated
that i would never get through medical school.
i had wanted to be a doctor my entire life since
i was little.
i had called my parents to tell them that i wanted
to quit.

i didn't feel like i had any hope.
i felt that i was failing at the one thing i had wanted
to do all of my life.
there was no point in living.

i sat on my twin bed in my apartment alone
with the hunting rifle across my thigh.

i took the bullets out of the box.
i kept thinking how my life was over.
i could not go forward and i could not go back.

i went back and forth in my mind about
how my life was over and i was a failure.
i was ruminating on my failure
and the hopelessness if i dropped
or failed out of medical school.

...

my phone rang. i answered. "hi, cheryl"
"hi," on the other side.
"do you want to go out to dinner?"
my best friend from medical school asked me.

i hesitated and then we made plans
to go out to dinner.

i put the gun back in the case
and put it back in the closet.
we went out to dinner.

i never told anyone for 15 years that
i had wanted to commit suicide.
i felt like a failure and ashamed.
i did not get any psychiatric help at that time.

my life was saved by someone
who just took the time to call me.
had she not stopped me,
there would not have been three children,
numerous lives impacted in a small town
in the midwest as a family physician,
and a plethora of acrylic paintings done in my life.

**if you ever feel
that one phone call won't make a difference,
i am a living proof that it does. "**

dr cheryl iverson

you were
never not enough,

i want you
to remember that

you are part of an imaginable big story;
you are not just enough,
but you are exactly what is needed in that story

forgive, it leads to freedom

forgiveness is how you cut the chains that tie you to who
and what wronged you
and it returns you back to yourself
your capacity, potential, audacity to be more
more than what happened to you or who happened to you

you don't need the weight of your past on the wings of your dreams
forgiveness creates both the path and freedom to return back to
yourself,

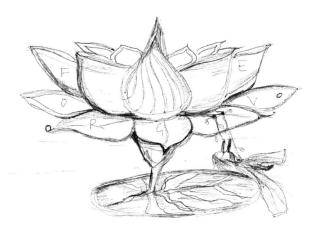

it brings back the focus to where it is needed- towards your growth
use it enough, use it massively, use it reflexively
it is the one superpower that everyone has. forgiveness liberates you
to become more than your pain, to become more than your past

when you forgive you create love and i want you to know
that's a very powerful thing

returning the taboo, that was never mine

i give myself permission
to be a person
who bleeds
certain days of the month
preparing a womb
in case i decide to
further procreate humanity,

and takes pride and not shame
in that most organic process
that has sustained
the entire species possible

so no, i am not going to be
made ashamed of that ever
no, i am not wrapping
my sanitary pads or tampons
when i buy them

and

i am not going to whisper
i need birth control
when i need it

...

your sense of judgement
over my own body is not welcome

i give myself permission to be a person who carries
breasts that can feed, so the beginnings of life
don't starve so the next time when you see me
taking care of my own child by breastfeeding in private
or in public, your synthetic boundaries of modesty will
bounce back from my sense of need to care for my child
...

i give myself permission
for not having it all or having it all
or wanting it all or not wanting it all

i give myself permission
to learn about self, passion or purpose,
to mock validation and rejection alike
to be not only ok with my finite self
of pain and pleasure, but celebrate my mortality
by not carrying
the weeds of regret in my mind
that prevent the garden of growth from flourishing
to laugh at milestones set by others
when my own bones are cemented
with their own ancient scriptures of dreams

i give myself permission
to celebrate the body that i am,
which has curves, and skin, and a body
that goes through changes in shape and size

which wants to celebrate itself
with intimacy or without intimacy,
with dance, mountain climbing, pregnancy,
or whatever makes it come alive

which wears however many tattoos it wants,
with or without piercings,
however long or short clothes she wants,

whether i run for an office, whether i write a book
whether i run a nonprofit, whether i create art,
whether i create family or choose marriage,

...

who can be sensuous if she wants,
a dress is not provocative,
your reaction to all of it is
and your reaction is your responsibility, not mine

rejecting your notion
that being desirable is my primary function
it is not-
it's to manifest the universe inside of me

i give myself permission to step outside
the four walls of
shame - honor- hesitation - judgement,
and take on the road of
growth- skills- learning and passion

to marry my truth
with no regard to
whether it makes you uncomfortable

towards healing, whether
the jagged margins of its process
are piercing your opinions of me
and bleeding your frames of reference

or to speak my story of assault or award when i am ready,
whether you are ready to hear it or not

i give myself permission to take new chances
irrespective of other's opinions
and at times fighting against
my own conditioning of inadequacies
for the heck of experience
and not the end results
...

i give myself permission
to value the experience and not beat
myself down every time there is a failure

i give myself permission
not to beat other women down
every time there is a failure
i refuse to worship or belittle others or myself,

i give myself permission
to grow, learn and experience
irrespective of the outcome, and to forgive

so i can make space for possibilities,
still making strong boundaries that i need

i give myself permission to be a person
i give myself permission to remove
the dates of expiry
from my dreams, my body, and my age

i give myself permission
to be free to be a woman and i am returning
all the weights of shame, labels- honor and caution
that you tied to my feet

because i need to fly

my wings need to build their own skies
my wings need to build their own skies

dedicated to Dambara Upadhyay

Dambara Upadhyay died from smoke inhalation in the hut, after lighting a fire to keep herself warm in cold weather.

She was compelled to sleep outside her safe home, because she was having periods, which is still a taboo in certain communities around the world

i have braided waves

in the ocean of pain
swirling my heart-

in beauty of water
in beauty of salt

i have braided waves
i have braided waves

in beauty of water
in beauty of salt

tsunami that i contain,
in the sea that i have become

healing and returning

you don't turn numb forever
that's like closing the door to life forever,

it's ok to stay inside closed doors
till you put your eyes back on,
your hair grows back thick,
till your ribs stop bleeding,
and the fire on your skin is extinguished,
till your bones feel strong enough
to cement back together
you can stay in close doors
so you can be ready
for the light that
you have forgotten,

you can stay numb till then
but not forever
you got to get ready for another war
for another fall
for another hiking on clouds
for another major mistake
and conquest,
you have to get ready
for the destiny that is you
you can't stay numb forever,

you are the playground
for love, life, pain, hurt and joy
you can't be forever under construction
unfold your purpose,
you don't turn numb forever

dedicated to dr anupriya grover

"during a mission trip to the dominican republic,
my roommate danielle noticed my bruised legs.
"-within five days of danielle's comment,
 i was diagnosed with acute lymphoblastic leukemia –
i was told that- i didn't have much time.

what happened over the following 13 months
is seared into my memory but one thing that i learned
from my experience was how powerful the feeling of
hope can be.

i lost my hair, my femininity, my fertility,
as well as the loved ones that suddenly became
uncomfortable with my diagnosis.

i didn't ask for these losses
and i had no say in how they happened.
i felt out of control with all the loss happening around
me that i lost hope with it. but my inner circle was there
to catch me as i fell deeper into it; they supported me
and loved me unconditionally and restored my hope.

in time, i saw the strength
that they saw in me first and began to believe
in my ability to heal again.
i began to see the losses as temporary
and knew that when i got better,
i would come back stronger and fiercer.
hope filled my heart again
and i found myself evolving in a way
that i never had, i entered remission on march 13, 2017. "

dr anupriya grover

it's not a race

once you realize
everyone and everything
is just visiting you,

you will learn
not to make a home outside of you

you will learn
that you don't
have to be brave all the time

you will realize
that you did build yourself
all these years

you grew tall
to see the world

and when you will crumble,
you will have new ideas
to rebuild yourself

you will realize
that finite life comes
with infinite possibilities

...

you will realize
the strength in tears and courage
in discarding fake smiles

you will realize that now is the
most powerful moment
and it belongs to only you

you will realize that when you stop
inflicting pain on yourself,

pain goes away
and peace comes in

you will realize that everyone and everything
is just visiting you

but the one that gets to stay with you
is the most glorious you

and you will realize that that's going to be enough

you are enough to create- a whole new you

i come with curves

you
can't
put
me in
a box

*an entire continent is exactly entire-
no apologies*

don't try to be relevant
try to be authentic
and
relevance will find you

say yes, to the depth, that you are

each moment is investing in you
you are a unique purpose in making

be patient, trust the process

post-traumatic stress syndrome,
trauma that stays

i ran to foreign sands
to bury things that shouldn't have happened
just to see them unbury, jump out, and be alive again

i poured out those things on paper
to leave them as words stitched
between ink and thoughts, but
they just cloned
themselves back in my throat

i begged the canvas for a final parting ritual
between me and them for vibrant colors
to take them all out of me
but alas they recoiled back from art to my inside

the more i left, the more i received
so now since no birth is possible
despite all the labor pains,
i carry them in my womb as part of me

i carry as they grow inside and outside of me and
i surrender to them
they write on me, they paint on me, they dream on me
no fire of dance can burn it
the immortality inside mortal being

i surrender to that
i surrender to the footprints of time
that never fade away

dedicated to dr kavetha sundaramoorthy

"my mom was married, via arranged marriage, to my dad,
when she was not even 16.
my heart aches when i look at their wedding pictures –
she looks so innocent, still in a child's body,
teenage acne adorning her face...
i came into their world when she was 17, and my dad was 30.

the family folklore goes that she would pinch me sometimes
when i cried as a baby, because she was so frustrated
and still a child herself.

when i was 18, she committed suicide.
the pesticide she drank quickly yellowed her skin.
when the doctor asked me to
'go see her for a few minutes,
we need to move her to the icu,"

i had the first sinking, nauseous feeling
that i associate with fear ever since.
i still remember the last moments we shared,
the words she said, the color of the wall,
the clothes she was wearing...
all of it. i didn't even have a word for it then.
i later learned it's called ptsd.

it took several years of learning, self-awareness,
discovery, practice, tweaking, and more learning.
slowly things started to fall into place.
the fog began to lift.

i went from feeling hopeless. to knowing how to live with,
and love another human being for life"

dr kavetha sundaramoorthy

her heart got fractured
and
light came out

defiance

i broke me
so i can adjust to the height
of your dreams

i trimmed my eyes
to match the vision
that your semi-clouded fear carried

i convinced me
that my flaws were bigger
than my hands that carried love

i tied my feet
so my wings don't take me anywhere

and with a half of me gone
with the other half of me,
which was full of you,

you left me
in the scorching desert of lies

...

now i am on an
adventure of stitching
me together
with my shaking hands,
i build me

and no i must not return to
the land where you were my god

with passion in my womb, i will bleed
and with burning salt in my bones
and the sun in my scars

i will carve a goddess out of me
i will carve purpose out of this pain
i will carve a temple from my ruins

you buried me deep in the earth
now you watch
as i come out as a
dense sandalwood forest

i am a woman,
even a half of me can create
more than full constellations

dedicated to dr pooja

"i stood again frozen, hearing my heart pounding,
as i feared for dear life just like every other time.
knowing very well he would charge at me
with clenched fists or anything he could grab at.
i got ready to take it all in. folding hands i pleaded
for mercy as my 2-year-old son watched silently.
my skin had ripped open to my skull

i got 13 sutures and drove back home,
couple days later i was in the middle of another attack,
the saga continued for 5 years
and i lost count of the bruises on my body.
he would plead sorry; i would forgive,
i stayed with a recurring thought- i am a successful woman
it could not be happening to me.

amidst the darkness, my long-lost dream
to become a physician stayed alive and i studied hard.
i did not have strength to walk away
and i endured in silence.
then came a night when he said he was taking my son
and there was nothing i could do to stop him.

i knew that moment if i did not act
then i would lose my son, may be forever.
i had to save him. soon i gathered all my courage
and ran away from my own home with my son.
leaving behind a broken marriage,
i entered medical school.
life was extremely hard, but i did my best.

here i am a physician finishing my training
and looking back at my incredible path.
there is so much more to life, to give, inspire,
and touch many lives as i continue along my journey."

dr pooja
(name changed for anonymity)

you thought you
killed me

like how they thought

darkness ate
the moon,

the eclipse is
not an ending

welcome to
my full moon night

you are not just phases, you are all of this, that, and then some more

darling
when you left me midair
thinking i will sink

you never noticed
my majestic wings

i see art
and i see music
and i see poetry

as proof that we are made of light

and when we let it pass
unfiltered and without
shadows of fear,

it radiates beauty for everyone

bravery is the force that allows the flow of universe through you

there were several words
that travelled across my tongue

and they paused, then jumped,
they rushed to burst out

but instead, they froze, on the dark snow
of shivering silence
in a long winter of fear

and now the sunshine of freedom
and the light of bravery
are warming them up,

and they dance out in flair and panache,
they decorate and flower themselves,
they simply pour out as poems

walk towards the freedom, to be you

when you love someone
in their good day
and
their absolute best

its convenience

when you love someone
when they are down
and without light

and you share your light
at the expense of
your own visibility for the path ahead

that's love, that's magic, that's everything

and the soul of the universe
taking shape in one beautiful action

true love is not always comfortable,
but it will always have abundance

peace is not a place or a person
or a thing around you
peace is making space for acceptance,
rest, and growth, and immersing in it
irrespective of the place,
event, or person, or thing around you

peace is acceptance

you may not
get everything
you desire in your life

but if you work
very very hard

you can become
the person
you always desired to become

and that's something
incredible to aspire for

the becoming

don't make me a goddess

don't make me a goddess
and put me in a temple
of brick and mortar

don't praise me for my quiet
or reward me for
repressing my every sense
and call my silence holy water

don't offer prayers for my caution
and tie weights of honor
to my mouth, skin and feet

don't make me a goddess
and keep me away from pious lands
when my womb
prepares for sustaining humanity

don't offer me shame
when i am fulfilling
the cycle of life

don't keep exhausting
scriptures over me

don't stitch limits
for my heart and soul
which you won't stitch for yourself

...

my tresses belong to the wind
my heart belongs to wild dreams
my soul traverses the route

that each of my cells has arranged with the sky

i am not going to offer you
cleansing of your veins
with the blood of my dreams

don't make me a goddess,
i wish to be free,

and that is my spirit of sacredness

my refrain is not your redemption

the wings on my feet
are not worried about your threat
to rob off the ground beneath me

you cannot take away who i am

transmitting ink from sky

what i write gives me shivers
but i must take my words
beyond the firewall
and i must pour ink
along with my flesh and my heart,

i must pour ink
along with my greatest fears and flaws,
i must pour ink along with
the threatening feeling
of being naked and truthful,

i must pour ink
despite getting disrobed, judged,
and revealed to eyes that can't see what i have seen,

i must pour ink
along with the pain of being presented,
pinned on pages that are more scared than fear itself

because when i pour ink and
when a half of me becomes words,
i feel rested and in peace because
now it's not just mine,
it belongs to everyone, to a collective consciousness

...

those who are still stitching themselves
together with shaking wings and trembling hands,

those who are posing questions
that others dare not,

those who are weeding out doubts
but don't see the distant tribe
doing the same,

those whose extraordinary ache
has replaced the blood in their veins,

i pour ink because someone,
somewhere carries a soul that will move
an inch back to life with just one drop of it

to baptize all that is lost
and all that will be found,

and so i must pour ink
and let it flood the pages

to reach parched eyes and dry, cracked hope

which are just a few words away
from the bloom they deserve

for that very reason, i must pour ink

never
stop growing

to accommodate anyone

however, endearing
the flowery bushes may seem,

the tree won't discover its purpose
if it stays stunted

keep growing,
all that belongs to you will find you,
and will stay

learn to love the height, that your soul needs you to be

all
the
stories
sprout
out

when

you rain
just the
right
words

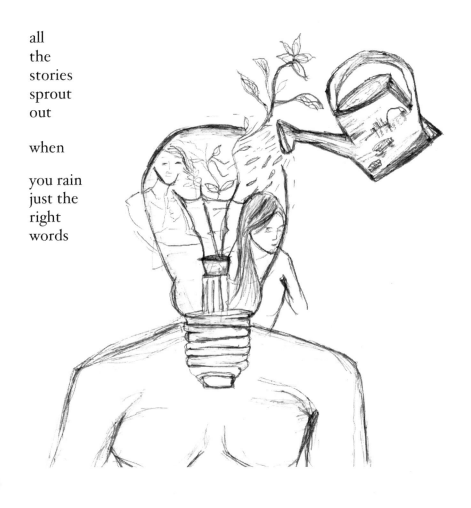

your wars are your unique stories
that no one else can claim

it's ok to be at war with things
that no one will know
you fight with all that is inside of you

not all battles make it to books
not all victories are sung
not all bloodshed of the soul
returns equal exchange of sacrifices and rewards

but all the bruises, will become art

all pain becomes poetry, all joys become colors
all the wrong done to you becomes wisdom

all the scars weave softness,
all hurt becomes compassion
all of the pride becomes introspection,

and all the hope becomes the foundation of
what massive city you will become,
and that's the unseen gift of those wars

happiness is not the absence of pain
but liberating a vast space of you in accepting
life in all its forms and celebrating that

when broken is as beautiful

some things are better left broken
half unfinished, incomplete, less than full

may you find poetry in such things
may you accept the beauty of such things

may you find a place in your heart
without the restlessness to change them

but to leave them as a muse

for often that's where art, music, colors
and songs come out,
the movement of life both begins and flourishes

may you find ways and grace
in your heart for imperfect beauty

in a world obsessed with completion, goals,
deadlines, measurements, comparisons,
perfection, having-it-all tales,

may you find the courage to celebrate them,
be them, and at times, become them

let's make a few sandcastles of love
 with no worry of the waves of time

say yes to nourishing moments

be an honest and loyal lover to yourself

somehow,
they have brainwashed you
into craving and validating
the love outside of you

from someone else
for someone else
from somewhere else
for somewhere else
and declared you guilty
if you dare do otherwise

let me set you free today
the happily ever after you truly need
is the one within you-
the one with yourself

i give you permission today
to fall in love with yourself
every single day
for no reason and every reason

i am joining you in that celebration
of the glorious one that you are

"once i posted a video of me dancing on instagram,
some man left a comment fat shaming me -

i was too tired to reply, and i removed the video
and then i thought why, why would i do that.

and then i posted the dance video again
with following comments on both instagram and facebook.

dear one,

my existence is taller than someone's opinion,
my meaning of life is massive and celestial
to be bothered by someone calling me anything.
i don't owe anyone any explanation for my life
or about my life for any reason.

but i thought of writing following piece
for the people that may be tempted to fatshame me
or anyone else in the future.

my body was not brought to the earth to be desired
by you or the likes of you, my body was brought
here in this planet as a vessel to manifest
dreams of the universe-
my body is always a work in progress
and is always loved by me.

...

it carries me to places, it helps to retain information
and then as a doctor, help save someone's life,
it helps me create words of comfort and hugs
to those who are struggling and silently suffering.

it dances to make me feel
one with the soul of the universe,
it has allowed me to experience events, people
and places, it creates art, so parts of the stardust in it,
can reveal their majestic glow.

i have experienced the beauty of touch
and learned warmth of wisdom through it.
it's magical enough to create another life out of
it if it wants. though at times it gets neglected by
me but there is no meaning of my soul without it
and vice versa.

while i recognize i need to keep it in optimal health,
to do all the justice to it,
for making this very life possible on this planet,
still it doesn't need 'shame' as motivation.

so, the person who was fat shaming me,
i don't hate you, we women inadvertently do that
enough to ourselves, in moments of frustrations
and weakness. i understand how we all get
brainwashed by images in media and concept of beauty

...

but my friend, people are not just inches or dresses,
or appearances people are the bouquet of stories-
interesting ones,

that is getting translated by their flesh
and you can learn a lot about their life
by not quickly judging them.

we all look different

because we are stories of multiple generations
and time prints, as we navigate through
several different paths of life.

so, to again reinstate
being desired by you or anyone else
is not why i am here,
to be inspired and to inspire and express the love
i am feeling constantly for the universe and its creations,
is why i am here.

and for my sisters out there doing their best,
no matter what size, shape or color you are,
dance away my love.
i am sending you my hug,
you are loved - those on magazine covers,
those reading them, those not reading them,
those whose stories are never read,
i am here to tell you - they are worth learning from."

you must
first travel within

yes
travel within you

before
you venture out

so even if you get lost outside,

you will have one address you always can return to,
you always can belong to

home that you carry within, home that carries you

i hope you meet poetry sometime somewhere in your life

i promise it will carry you
even when the whole of you can't

words that can become your legs, words that can become your wings

relationship status

i am in a relationship
with my body, mind and soul

i am in a relationship
with learning about their needs-
their optimum status

i am in a relationship
with learning the universe around me
and being in sync with it

i am in a relationship
with joy, growth, breaking,
healing, dreams, goals

i am in a relationship
with the sun and the moon
and the breeze that settles
newness in my soul

i am in a relationship
with the people around me that augment me

i am in a relationship
with making boundaries to keep out
those that empty me

i am in a relationship
with this love i experience
constantly of just being,
and all of this is beautiful

the relationship that fuels me back

i am trying to raise myself
to parent
a rebellious heart and
a soul
that is bigger than a storm

i need gods
in my hand and iron
in my thoughts

soul harvesting

come let's go

every single goodbye
that you did not want,

wanted for you
to go back to your own city
or to a new city,
and light a few more towns,
say hi to a few more people

become a few books,
travel on new canvases
notice your wings, dive in new oceans,
surf new skies, plant new gardens

every single goodbye
is turning you towards
several million hellos and hugs
towards several million lives
waiting to happen
both inside and outside of you

so please welcome every single goodbye

as a gateway to much much more of you
as a gateway to much much more for you

  people seek anchors
because no one told them about the wings
      that grew on their back,
so big and beautiful all these years

true elegance lies
not in building yourself
so, you can look better than
others but so you can better
others
and therefore, yourself in the process

what success is

i am under construction
and i love it

don't worry they said
one day
you won't be broken anymore

why should i strive for
less than an extraordinary travel
i shrugged in peace

my greatest adventure came out
when cracks appeared on me and
i get to enter inside of me
and then more doors opened
and i travelled more inside of me

you want to glue me back together
so i am easier
on your eyes, ears, skin, hands,
and finite mind

...

non-threatening, less awake,
unaware of the world inside of me,

buying what you sell me,
the idea of everything right,
packaged in acceptable success

enough grace, enough beauty
enough words, enough questions,
just enough, nothing more, nothing less

i won't close any door
that takes me closer
to the soul of me
that world has my address,
sorry you can't post me letters there

i am making new words
new ink, new me, new everything,

as i lie here in pieces
i have never felt more complete

where learning exists, suffering does not

you have that glow they whispered,

yes,

i have a thousand splendid undying suns
that roar in my veins

they crash into each other
in every breathing moment

you see the soft morning light,
i feel the undying eternal burn

i swallow their rough heat
so i can deliver their soft light for all of your mornings

the passion that i carry

pain will arrive early
learning will arrive late,

amidst that is a space
and life meets you there

from the book - pillow of dreams

you are the owner of two superpowers

ability to create thoughts
and ability to act on them

may you know them
and may you use them well

decisions are the gods that you carry
and gods that carry you

i will never dismiss your ache
by mentioning the sufferings of someone else

my respect does not come with measuring cups for tears

let yourself rain,

you carry too much in you – let yourself rain

cry when you need to
let the river in you find its ocean, let it break the dam

let it out,

the dance in your soul,
stretching through your
ribs,

let it out

don't hide your glory

do not lead her on

if you are gonna just pass by,
let her know
where the path leads you,
let her know the stories of the truth
and wisdom of the destinations you undertake,

don't tell her she is your home
when your journey has just begun,
or is unfolding itself,

and you are still learning
about the lands in sight,
and those out of sight,

give her inspiration, not promises,
show her friendship and respect,
not words without meaning

because what you leave with her
will find you,
whether lies or betrayal or deceit,
you never leave them with the person,

but they grow legs
and they grow in size
as children of your actions,

...

and they will return
all the gifts that contained
more ache than a person
can pay in one lifetime

so,
if you are gonna just pass by,
let her know
where the path leads you,

let her know
the stories of the truth,
and the wisdom
of the destinations you undertake

don't tell her, she is your home
when your journey has just begun

karma is a goddess

some losses will be your biggest gains
don't crowd your hands with regrets,
let us make space for all the blessings

leave the past where it belongs, in the past

at times the one you need saving from is

'you'

every time you put yourself second
every time you said yes when you wanted to say- no

every time
you put your heart
into the mouth of the dragon that he was

every time you shame
your body, your dreams, your mistakes

make that enemy go away
by making yourself a friend to you

stop inflicting hurt on your soul,
you deserve a better version of yourself, make one

and you are assigned to spend
all of your water
outside to quench their thirst

you do this
with little fires collapsing your own soft parts inside
allow yourself to address the drought
inside of you first

replenish

when you can't find
the one,
you become that example

the power to invent and then re-invent yourself

the depth in me came from drowning
massive water that i never wanted
became the water that i always needed

the one
you have been waiting
for all along to rescue you is

'you'

the biggest power lies within

you are the knight, the armor and the roaring army,
you are it all

allow yourself
to be not a superhero at times

allow yourself
to be ok with celebrating what is an ordinary moment

allow yourself
to accept hurt and pain
as the most human part of this experience called life

allow yourself
pause -to not be anything- for as long as you need

allow yourself
to be not in competition with fellow human beings
but in collaboration with them

allow yourself
to encourage kids that are not yours with
the same vigor and grace as they will teach your kids
more than what you will teach them

allow yourself
to have days where perfection takes a backseat
and authenticity and being real is all you need

....

allow yourself
bravery- and not the results-
if you want to indulge in your dreams

allow yourself
to uplift other women, communicating,
and not assuming their intent or action

allow yourself
to see the beauty of time and living-
in the stretch marks and folds on your tummy

allow yourself
to see a messy home as a well-lived home
and not a project

allow yourself
to sit back and make a cup of tea
and say it out loud –

i may never get this life thing entirely,
but right now, i am sending love vibes
to everyone including myself

allow yourself
grace of failures and gifts of setbacks,
sprinkles of little joy, and a hot cup of tea
whenever you can

grant yourself a lot of grace

let your heart
guide you
your mind will find
the way

follow your passion

messages become lessons
when the student is ready

roads become reasons when you are ready

i am leaving behind

a trail of words,

in case i can't find me again

your soul is your home

what you allow will enter

what you allow will stay

ownership

how not to be cruel to yourself
will be the most important thing

you will need to learn in this lifetime

how not to be cruel to others
will become an extension of that learning

i wish people can see
how breaking
can become
a beautiful art-form

a broken glass
can become a majestic chandelier
with the glue of self-love
and the light of vision within

breaking is how the soul stretches to discover itself,
to expand itself, to make itself and to remake itself

movement that life is

moving on is scary
but it's more scary than necessary,
that's a lie we feed ourselves

we divorce something or someone
but we stay married to the pain
that we have learnt

we think if we stay there,
it's familiar and less fearful
than an unfamiliar pain

so, we stay
till the decay becomes deeper
than the roots that we grew all these years

and we still stay refusing to admit

that the tree of our life
no matter how many bright flowers bloomed,

...

how many birds arrived,
came, and celebrated,

how many lives fed on its fruits

without roots,
it is not a tree
but a fancy temporary
bark with a short-lived life

but what if one day
you remembered oh how tall,
oh, how magnificent you are

taller than fear,
stronger than darkness,
and you leave
the old pain
for new challenges

and you keep the learning
to use new pain
when it visits
to make you even taller

....

moving on is not scary,
it's a necessity
so blood can keep running
through the veins of your life

forward upwards, forward upwards
forward upwards, forward upwards

making boundaries is part of love

you have the right

to move away from negativity

you have the right to remove people
from your life when their agenda changes

you have the right to add people in your life
who are uplifting to you and others-

that is a freedom towards growth

to forgive doesn't mean
you have to give the precious space
that can be occupied by someone
who nourishes your soul

to someone who has an otherwise intention

life is too short to explain yourself
trust your gut, your glory awaits you

if you have to wonder
about someone's intentions,
that's the universe giving you signs

move away when you need to,

no one deserves you more than you

practice pause

you don't have to carry things heavier than your hands
all the time
learn to put them down

and do
the dance of lightness

your hands need to breathe air once in a while too

towards the end,

you will realize it was not about the finish line,
it was all about the beauty of that dance

*even nature created autumn to celebrate resetting itself
and making the process become beautiful*

soul of the woman

disperse me gently like jazz in the air
make a temple out of my ruins

let my each curve heal softly,
make a prayer out of all my sighs

silk my breathing and pour me on flowers,
make a goddess out of my shadow

weaving scriptures out of my pious periods,
claim a woman out of this flesh

make a name from thrown-out syllables,
let me come back to you, inhale me deep

and let me breathe deep in your womb,
and then disperse me again like jazz in the air

from existing, to knowing, to learning, to manifesting

*your purpose in life, is an alive and breathing interface
between you, divinity in you and the universe*

you must begin with love

we all are so tempted to hide behind
the so-called perfect life that
we forget to hug our truth and
fall in love with our reality

we are sold shame for being different
and we buy that shame for being different
we leave joy despite its truly being ours
because we are taught that we need to be
certain something and someone to have that joy

who are these people that have authority?
and power over our dignity and joy? and why

or all of that is an illusion
and we submit ourselves to that illusion
that ridiculous authority till we die

i was having this conversation with a person
i met recently, and i wanted her
to hear this loud from me
till it cements in her bones and echoes in her soul
every time someone makes her feel ashamed
and i think it helped her, i hope it helped her.

so, there was a picture of a woman
in the bathing suit being joyful at the beach
and there was a twitter war over this argument
the gillette was supporting
a woman with an unhealthy body

...

why is celebration, joy, and dignity being the right of only a few
and who is selling that right.
who owns that equity,
and we rent them out when we are deserving?

they are selling us what we already have and is rightfully ours.
as per 'them'
we should remain miserable and ashamed
till we achieve that perfection in ever-changing
and forever changing life, body, and situation.

so, when we go to our deathbed,
we carry so much inside of us that it's heavier than our grave.
this is why this image is so powerful and important
and all men and women or any gender should understand.

to hell with that dictatorship of brainwashing.
you do not need to suffer in order to chase your dreams.
you do not need to be hard on every single moment
that is wanting to meet you where you live waiting
to glorify that other moment that is yet to arrive
or is in the making. you do not need to be angry at yourself
when you did not deliver all that is right or when you fall down.

you deserve joy, peace, calm, ambition, fulfillment,
passion, happiness and motivation at any stage of life and

those who tell you that, they don't award you with any of that.

then you straighten your crown and leave those words
where they came from and walk towards the glory that you are.

...

you are not some project or deadline or imaginative waiting.
you are an ocean beaming with life
every moment of every hour of every day.

the wait is over, and the delusion is over.
you are your destiny - own it,
and love, love, love, love, yourself –
without a darn need of waiting.

how do i judge you

when i find myself
constantly evolving and changing

how do i not forgive you when
i wish to be forgiven by so many

allow redemption for others to receive redemption for self

love does not hurt,
greed does
and somehow greed always enters,
always enters

to end the beginnings of a few fairytales

but i want you to know
what died with such heartbreaks
was supposed to die

and what is born after that
is the glory of something incredible

go through the conception,
the labor pain of delivering
the best version of you,
it's worth a million heartbreaks

be born, be patient, be a learner, be brave

hardships give you the gifts that you need, not the ones you want

between most sunrises and sunsets,
most extraordinary moments
turn mundane
because you choose fear over love,

it does not have to be this way

when
someone
wrongs you,
the best revenge is

to do something
for your growth
that day and the
day after and

then every single
day thereafter

and to help
someone who
cannot

churning compassion for self and others,
out of the pain that you received, is the greatest gift to the world

uncertainty is the friend of creativity

you should prepare
for adventures
instead of the safe place

the only promise life makes
is that of 'experience'

there is no winning
there is no failing,

there is only experiencing

success & failures are societal things,
milestone things,

now how you experience,
and what you want to experience

if you are building
or creating something,

deliver your best

...

because your dreams choose you,
your passion chooses you,
because you have it in you
to manifest them

during this,
things at times will go your way
and at times teach you other ways

that's pretty much it,

so follow your heart
and do it with humane integrity

and attach it to a purpose
higher than yourself
after meeting your survival

that's what
you owe to the universe
for bringing you here,

 you must make peace with that

a too much woman

your eyes slip on my curves

and then you try to catch
the meteors bursting through my skin
you dive into my thoughts and
fail to recognize any creatures
that you come across

you see the untied noose
between pain and shame
in a corner of my pride,

you see the glory of wrecks
amidst cities of flowers

you witness
the dance in my throat
and the riot in my mouth

you see the poise in my touch
and the revolution in my words

you see me spin
gold from my
suffering and calm
from my art

...

you see a festival
when you thought
you were entering to sit through
a predictable event

you see extraordinary
but you don't speak that language
you sort through all your labels
and you find no name
in your given designated alphabet

and you nail it on my forehead
'too much a woman'

you are right, sir

i am meant

to be celebrated
not understood,

not yet

to be a woman

is to be several things at once
and i will never blame you sir,
for being none of them

stay rooted in love
stay rooted in love
stay rooted in love

no storm of hate
is long enough
or strong enough

to move
such a forest of wisdom

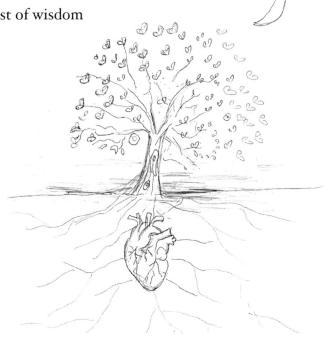

love conquers it all, love will save us all–
choose love, know love and be love

you are not defined
by your tragedies

but you are defined
by what you do
while you are inside of them
and after them

you are defined by
what you become
and who you become

when there is darkness
you are not only defined
by how well you harvest light from nothing

but by sharing your light
no matter how scarce it may seem
at that point of time

tragedies are where you can birth newness

don't eat your own voice
don't eat your own voice
don't eat your own voice

all those
who tell you to do so
will not be carrying
the storm
of the violence
in their own belly
of what
you had to say all along

SPEAK
UP

before the flesh returns to the sand,
you must return all your words to the world

if you can't reach my soul,
you can't reach my skin

you can't meet me at the surface
you will need to drown to my depth to breathe with me

in my arms there is enough lush softness

beneath my skin
there are wars that were fought to save & rescue it

scars that guard my softness

i am less than you,
because you have decided so

i sit here looking like,
you know, not one of you

you glanced at my record
you familiarize yourself
with names that have been
assigned to me
my twentieth visit with unexplainable pain
and fatigue and other symptoms

you have decided
i am less than you and so my pain
is also less than you

because you cannot find
an answer for my issues
so, my issues must not exist,
my pain should not exist

because your few standard diagnoses
don't accommodate that spectrum,
i become a functional patient
who barely can function in her real life

...

as i struggle with the pain
that i never invited
as i lose my lung
to catamenial pneumothorax,

you do not accept
your lack of knowledge of my condition
instead, you hide behind your tall ego
and sentence me as a crazy patient

but your calling me names
did not help me
drug seeker, histrionic, liar, hypochondriac, somatoform,
still did not help me
i take in all the pain in that i had never invited

one fine day after years of a stolen life,
one willing doctor finally tells me
i have endometriosis

whom do i ask to return my youth
that i had instead spent
on my education, sports,
romance and just being carefree

...

whom do i ask to return the time
that had left me with
much less of it

so the next time
when your vanity decides
i am less than you,
and your ego decides my origin of my suffering,
if you don't know, it should not exist

when you are about to tell a woman,
she is histrionic and attention-seeking,
pause, pause, pause
and then go back to your books
and reread and relearn

because that's not
what a good physician is supposed to do,
but what a good person is supposed to do

what you write in your chart
will become
the story of me for the rest of my life

   ...

so, pause
before your callousness dismisses
my truth and insults me
as a villain of my own story

maybe think, believe,
and research, and consult

before the chain reaction
of the disbelief in my story starts
with your one simple statement
and spreads like wildfire
all across medical records,
think, learn, acknowledge,

before you dismiss
your fellow human being and their suffering
when their flesh does not function like yours

it doesn't make me less than you,
it gives you an opportunity to help me,
you can't share my pain
but maybe you can solve my pain

pause, think, learn, help,
and more importantly,
believe in my suffering

dedicated to mimi, silvia, selma, susan and several women
whose symptoms are dismissed for the reason of gender or race bias

"a physician thought i had munchausen because she'd not
seen idiopathic central adrenal insufficiency before.
the other (at a national referral center) wanted to simply
adjust my treatment for hypoglycemia when it recurred
after 2 years and would have missed adrenal insufficiency.
i had to suffer a long time and was dismissed several times
despite being a physician myself, before my diagnosis
was made."

dr mimi emig

"it seems like a lifetime of seeking medical help, wanting
someone to care. deaf ears, cynics and no one believing my
symptoms, an er physician was about to discharge me home,
till i insisted to get me a ct scan of abdomen which confirmed
my suspicion of small bowel obstruction, he assumed
i am a pain medication seeker because at home, i am on pain
medications for spinal stenosis."

dr susan hoffman

"alone in the center of the room, that's how i feel,
encaged and enraged. banging my head until i bleed,
but it's fruitless. i learn to reign it in, i learn to act well,
but it's draining my energy to pretend.
because how do you prove yourself when the system
undermines your witness. i was diagnosed with endometriosis
after years of struggle to be heard, i had a lung collapse
because of endometriosis and no one paid attention to why.
they just did not believe me."

silvia wheatley young

you keep telling
the stories soaked in tears

till the tsunami in you dries
up, i promise it will dry up.

let it rain

the massive mist you carry, part water, part salt, part stardust,

my
poetry
is the
voice
of several million women,

whose words
and feelings
have not met
yet

i put their
storms in
syllables

so, the
violence
that they
feel

can churn
outside their
belly for once

freedom via the revolution that are words

i don't see your rage,
i see a lot of pain,
dressed up as anger,
come drown in me,
your fire meets the water here

somewhere today

somewhere a woman chose to be sensuous
somewhere a woman chose to be maternal
somewhere a woman chose to be a leader
somewhere a woman chose to be a lover

somewhere a woman allowed herself to break down
somewhere a woman allowed herself to stay longer
than what others believe is ok to be broken

somewhere a woman decided to laugh out loud
with her friends and dance away the day

somewhere a woman allowed herself
feeling lonely and cry her salt water out
somewhere a woman decided to step out of her
loneliness and try this thing called life all over again

somewhere a woman allowed herself
sexuality with pride and not taboo
somewhere a woman allowed herself
to be asexual with pride and not taboo

somewhere a woman decided to pick herself
from a depth much much below any rock bottom

somewhere a woman decided to quit her job
and be lost
somewhere a woman decided to stay
in darkness till she grows her legs and eyes back

...

somewhere a woman decided to declare
her bright beautiful wings stitched how many
more times and head for the sky
somewhere a woman is falling from the same sky
with burnt wings

somewhere a woman decided to forgive herself
somewhere a woman decided to forgive someone else

somewhere a woman is setting herself new goals
somewhere a woman is failing on the goals she set
somewhere a woman is victorious with what her goals are

somewhere a woman is doing her best
to just get through the day
somewhere a woman is not doing her best
but is just breathing to exist and be unclear for now

somewhere a woman is trying hard to not judge
other women or compare herself to others
somewhere a woman just started
a thousand times again after losing it again

somewhere a woman decided to support
all those women no matter
where they are and how they are.

because at some point in your life
you will be or may be one of those women

and even if you never are one of those women
you decided to share your light because

it's darn time to burn bright with all that we have

i paint because

i know
some stories
would burn the ink
eat the paper
and shiver the notes of any songs

so those stories
are better poured,
stitched, and hidden
between canvas and colors,

for the right eyes
carrying the exact same stardust
will actually find peace
in that violence of art

that's why i paint

stories that birth art

art adopted me
when the ground below

orphaned my soul

allow yourself slowness

and when you are
surrounded by
more reasons to feel

you are not enough
and you are not doing enough,

hug yourself tight,
touch your bones, teeth and hair,
taste the fresh breath in your mouth,

feel the glory in being alive,

embrace the universe
feeding you
with sun, water, soil,
plants, starry nights and what not

you are allowed
to be frail, strong,
weak, injured

you are glorious
in all your forms

so, pause, breathe, and

share a smile, share a tear
share a hug or share nothing

...

not all days need to be awake
and need to be alive and accounted for,

a few days are to die
and be burnt into the making of nothing

pause breathe pause breathe

stroll, it's not a race, it's not a race

what is yours
is traveling to you.
you are the destination
of your destiny

earn yourself
before
you spend yourself,

rest before you walk

it's not a race, it never was

when you are tired

it does not mean you are not strong
but it means you are trying,
and you are moving towards something

and that's incredible
you are incredible

rest, recover, re rise & rejoice

"take your time "

you hold onto joy
you hold onto pain

they won't have roots
till you water them

who are you watering today

hello beautiful

when i call you beautiful
i am not talking about your hair
or clothes or the fresh fragrance
that you wear
or that perfect makeup

i meant the soul
that went to war
that it never wanted
and returned back
with both struggle and pride

i meant the smile
that you share
even when you are buried
under massive pain,

or the support that you give
even when uncertainty
pulls away the ground beneath your own feet

when i call you beautiful
i acknowledge your being a person
of both kindness and courage

who brings light and shines
through any darkness
when i call you beautiful
i admire your softness
amidst thorns and rocks,
...

i worship your belief that
despite given a million reasons not to,
why you should not love,
you bring out one sacred shrine of existence
and continue to hang onto the only prayer
that makes life worth living- the prayer of love

when i call you beautiful,
i want for you to remember that no matter,
how many cycles of new faces appear on new magazines,
your compassion will always be relevant

so, stay beautiful my beautiful

setting fire to the forest that eats us

i once met a man who told me how thick my arms
were and how if i lose 40 pounds i won't have to work
a day in my life because he was a successful doctor-
all i needed to do was look like a model that happened
to be a doctor.

he mentioned with no care for anyone in the world
how repulsive curvaceous women are.

i remember having dinner with him during that
conversation where he attempted to dissect my face
and the rest of my body giving me assignments to fix
the other things.

he scored my face and hair a ten and rest not so much,
he was generous with my arms.

what a sigh of relief to get approval from a man of his
stature, whose life goals were to accumulate expensive
cars and present me as a trophy wife.

his kindness that he wishes to marry me despite
my history of stroke, my invisible disability
which never existed,

he told me he emailed my doctor what my future risk of
stroke was to see if i am worthy of matrimony.

...

his affirmation that my lighter color will appeal to
his grandmother and family very much so,
while he himself was rich with dark melanin.

 i wish he had revealed that part of him on day one
instead of burning my days into nothingness.

i was mentally checked out within his first statement
and then became an amused audience of seeing him
like a disaster in very slow motion, revealing what
'ugly' actually is- cruelty, callousness and disregard
for the other half of the population.

i did not find it funny- that was my first introduction
to how education is not equal to class, understanding and
compassion.

i stayed in that conversation to know the underbelly of
a certain big segment of the opposite gender.

i walked away with grave concerns- those who know of me
know that i am an immovable mountain of self-assurance
deep inside; since as a child, not even those in obvious authority
had caused me ever to taste self-doubt.

but what about other women, young girls, who don't have the
armor of self-knowledge, weapons of self-assurance, tenacity of
self-worth

...

and purpose and pride that comes from knowing how
beautiful and unique each one is. it extended my
compassion immediately to women who suffer from eating
disorders, women who end their lives because they are
misled and conditioned into thinking that being desirable
is their only goal in life.

so, let me tell you what ugly is.

ugly is the blindness that enslaves the human race
that all need to look and be a certain way just to merely exist
and demand their rights from society they are born into
without their consent.

  that's ugly

poetry was my boat

when everything was nothing

but deep water

you are not damaged
you are a queen who braved through wars
and has the proof of valor
on her skin, soul and bones

you are the one who lived and conquered
or are in the middle of it all

that's rich- wholesome and not damaged

don't let them belittle your journey

you keep on and you stay
with your mighty head high, heart of lioness

queen that crowns life

why i write

i am not writing to house my words
or for providing a safe haven to my feelings
or for packaging my hurt
in a glitter of syllables
or for my pain
to lie there on pages for eternity

i am writing so that
some fragments of my thoughts can stay immortal
so, they can reach
a young girl in doubt
a woman in whirlwind
a man in chaos or joy

to feel their feelings,
dreams, and their experiences
as valid, shared, thought-before,
belonged, reckoned, connected felt
and understood

by so, so many others

...

i write to remove the inches of gap
laid down by the civilization
to dissolve boundaries
marked down by those
who benefit from them

i write because i know
words, art and music
can outlive death,
several kingdoms, and civilizations

i write because
i have walked on
legs of brave words,
i was pulled
by the strength of a poem

when a billion minds
share that thought,
to be that poem,
that becomes a constant reminder
that all hearts beat the same

i write for that

she went in straight
        for the eye of the storm
    and whispered,

    'my chaos is just as wild'

make fire out of your fears

there are things that
you say to yourself
that can destroy you

more than any army can
more than any hurricane can

there are things
that you say to yourself
that can save you
from any army from any hurricane

and at times even from you

what are you saying
to yourself today

what have you convinced
yourself of today

words that can make or break you

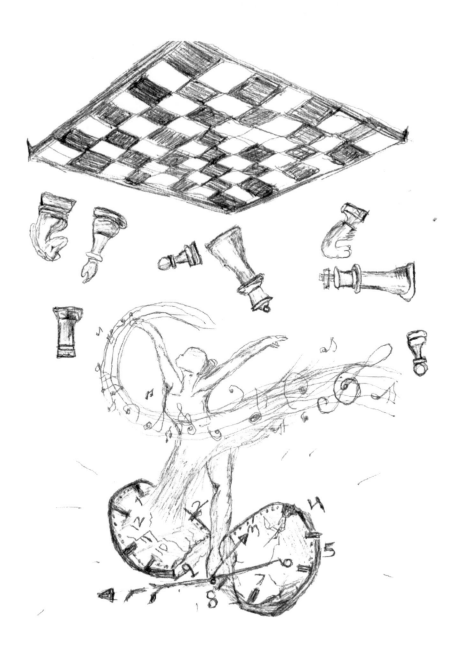

i have made peace with my chaos

dear unborn child of a billion-year-old stardust

some day when you begin to put words together and
read them out loud to yourself, they will make some
long-lasting pathways in your mind and will eventually
become a belief.

i want for you to be both aware of and awake to this fact.
please do remember that all those stories,
even when embedded in truth, at times may not
reveal all dimensions- other than
the beginning, middle and conclusion.

fascination with a 'single story' can preclude openness
of the mind. every time you approach a situation
with your belief, remember this bias.

it's important because your life in the world
will never be a single- story event.
life is never linear but rather has more dimensions
than our senses are taught or can comprehend.

remember to apply these principles before you judge yourself
or others with the yardsticks of your own beliefs

-are you aware of all the dimensions
-are you awake to all the meanings
-are you applying an open mind to comprehend them,
the easy example is-
you will be told a single story of a soulmate
- a simple fairytale-
some prince comes with his army to rescue you;
monster is slayed, and victory is celebrated.
but in real life, here is what you need to remember,

let's begin.
...

1- soulmates

soulmates are not just people or a person that's married to you
or courts you; they are not bound by forever.
at times they will be strangers that will help you for no reason
at times they will come in the form of love
at times they will come in the form of friendship
at times they will come in the form of time, coincidences
and at times they will come in the form of rejection- failures
and criticism. whatever or whoever takes you towards a better
version of yourself is a soulmate.
and if you don't fight them with your set expectations,
you can celebrate for however long they stay and
receive the gift they carry for you and if you stay open to all
experiences, they will lead to a change within you that you
always needed.

2- monsters

in real life the biggest monster to harm you will be your own self.
people don't do things to you; people do things for themselves.
and when you accept the unwanted upshots of their choices
and carry them in your life, it's you, it's you, and remember,
it's you who accepted those things to harm you.
and when that happens, remember you say it out loud to yourself.

oh darling, when you said, i can't- i left those words,
where they belong and walked towards the glory that i am,

make sure you know you have that authority all the time.
when you are spending your existence for experiences
without earning yourself back-
that's how you dwarf your existence, that is how you empty yourself.

...

earn yourself everyday-
growing centrally by exercise, meditation, introspection of self,
holistic nutrition, hydration, education, skills and forgiveness.
growing horizontally by
surrounding yourself with positive people, fulfilling relationships,
joy, good habits and forgiveness.
growing vertically by alignment of the body, soul, mind,
purpose, passion and understanding of the universe,
its life currency and forgiveness.

3- role models and worship

those who suffer don't carry innocence all the time, those
that inflict suffering are not always monsters.
everyone is capable of doing something great even when
they have proven otherwise
and everyone is capable of doing something horrible
even when their past has been contrary.
so, don't have role models but have role model actions
because this will let you hold people accountable- even when
they are treated like gods or heroes by the rest of the world.

and this will let you be tolerant and give people a
second chance even when they have been demonized by all.
being objective towards this fact will make it easy for
you to forgive and be rational at the same time.

4.undiscovered greatness is still greatness

every single story you will read, will have a beginning, middle,
and end. but in real life, there are more stories with
more segments and parts than there are papers, ink, or writers.
there are stories yet to be written. just because only a few
are celebrated doesn't mean others are not valid
so, when your life and achievements are validated,
stay humble and remember.
...

being discovered is not the greatest achievement
but being authentic is.

making some part of your life about uplifting
another life is the single greatest achievement.
just remember there are undiscovered geniuses,
and i hope once you excel, you do your bit in dissolving
the barriers keeping them from getting manifested.
also, anytime you are about to judge someone else
for the choices they make, remember,

familiar is not always right, different is not always wrong.

every experience is valid, resist the impulse to consider
yourself better than others because
people are free to be their unique version, and
everyone is an expert of their unique experience.
so, when you are about to say something about someone,
don't, unless it involves concerns for their safety
or unless it's about celebrating them or learning from them.
people are emperors of their choices, and
that's the freedom of life, liberty, and pursuit of happiness.

5. celebrate every moment

if you only wait to celebrate the conclusion of the
stories of your life, you will miss most of your life.
none of the stories prepares us for the poetry we will become.
learn to celebrate the process.
the ups, the downs, celebrate everything and everyone
even if no one else validates it, joy is always in fashion,
don't postpone your joy.
the currency of joy is important to garnish as much as possible.
it returns interest as hope and during challenging times,
it will take you forward.
if you stay authentic, it will find you- and you will experience
exhilarating bliss. i have always believed certain joys are in
your destiny and they will find you no matter what.

...

6.always be in love

as you will enter and immerse in life you will realize,
there are various forms of love-
the one that comes with intimacy, the one that comes with
an understanding of the self and life, the one that enters in
your life as purpose, or just the love of being alive,
always be in love and stay there.
it will give you inspiration
universe breathes in you as love
and you breathe it out in the form of creativity,
whether it's creating a life, art, memory, relation, experience,
or innovation
it happens when you are in love with something,
someone in some form, whether
it's an idea or purpose or person or passion.
so always be in love and stay there

7.don't judge others' ways of life

however, people choose to be happy, if it's not hurting you,
let them have a blast, also join in their celebrations if you can.
if wearing purple teeth makes them happy, let it be.
judgement is a heavy, unnecessary burden.

8.it's not the end of anything

as soon as humans are born, desires are born,
and they act as commands to the universe and of the universe.
release some incredible commands,
imagine how powerful your thoughts are. use them well,
and then you will fulfill your desires in this lifetime and
while pursuing them all the karma you collected will have its
extension in the next life, and the residual desires will create
another algorithm for the following lives.
universe grows and changes itself through you.
...

flesh is not supposed to contain soul but emanate the soul
and when it has manifested its purpose, it rediscovers itself
back in the form of another flesh and restarts next life.

you are part of a massive wavelength of
- universe- time- space- energy- mass, continuum,
you are one of little ripples creating another ripple
and major impacts during a very short lifetime.

9. admit to what you need

admission of your own flaws and weaknesses
will take you towards a most incredible journey
you will be your biggest investment, so grow,
learn about yourself and then build yourself up and up,
also make that process fun
suffering is destructive, pain, however, is constructive,
acceptance of pain and beginning of learning
is the end of all suffering.
pain is a university that can teach you a lot, if you let it.
that is the ultimate wisdom to conquer the self,
no matter where you are and who you are.
learning and growth are the holy water that vanquishes
the fire of suffering. starve your fears by massive actions

10.learn to reset

there are no endings, there are only new beginnings,
and more beginnings, and more beginnings.
you have this extraordinary capacity to reset, restart,
and reconstruct life, now give yourself permission to use that.
you cannot create change or any change without changing
your present and what you are at present.

...

remember endings become new beginnings if you let them,
and work on them. start, and then start over, and then you
will fall, you stay-rest-recover-then start over, start over
as many times as you need stay fallen as long as you need
and then start again. if things don't change, you don't change-
if you don't change things don't change.

11. self-assurance & actualization

they are the root of courage and courage is the root of living an
authentic life, and living an authentic life means to be in sync
with your soul, and to be in sync with your soul means
knowing your purpose-passion- pleasure, and knowing your
purpose-passion- pleasure, is the root of effortless peace and
a state of joy, and that is the fuel for further self-assurance and
actualization.

as society changes, traditions change, as traditions change,
expectations change, but these really are outward effects.

aiming for a traditional life can lead to several conflicts,
and at times interfere with growth.
however, self-assurance can open doors to a terrific life
which may or may not be traditional.

self-assurance leads to ultimate freedom from being
validated by external factors and people and opinions-
while you will value what others have to say and label-
your inner soul and heart will remain your guiding force and
compass, and your body and mind will help you accomplish
it effortlessly.

...

12. failure

there is no winning there is no failing- there is only experiencing
- success and failures are societal thing- milestone things,
not how you experience and what you want to experience.

if you are building or creating something, deliver your best,
because your dreams choose you, your passion chooses you,
because you have it in you to manifest them.

during this, things at times go your way and at times will teach
you other ways- that's pretty much it.

 follow your heart and do it with humane integrity
and attach it to a purpose higher than yourself.
after meeting your survival, that's what you owe
to the universe for bringing you here.

and remember no experience will enter the soul
that has closed its gate against growth-
stay open to learning,
for example, travel has the power to separate you from yourself
and then align you in ways you never can understand,
but you will know how to celebrate.

13. say no to the box- explore, learn, unlearn, create, think, and act.

at times people will put you in boxes that they know about,
their minds run based on set algorithms,
they match you as data with what is taught to them or what
they have experienced.
it takes awareness and not just education to be open-minded,
keep a space available for discussion of something unexpected.
since the unexpected usually triggers fear,
like how conventional usually triggers comfort.
through this lifetime, this is what conditioning is all about.
this is exploited by marketing and media.

...

those that step out of this trap have freedom for new
thoughts and those new thoughts can lead to new actions,
and such actions can create ripples which eventually can
at times change the course of humanity.

14.perfection

we don't need more perfection in the world,
we need more bravery,
we need more kindness, we need more tolerance,
we need more acceptance.

15- know your truth

there is always an option, time, and opportunity
to know your truth. start from there and flourish.
that's the only place for your roots to create all of you

16- eventually you will cease to exist

but what all you did prior to that may remain forever.
so, make something nice of the time before then
and have fun doing that.
your flesh will perish, your words will stay,
your impact will stay.

learn to take things sincerely not seriously,

wear orange and yellow and red and bright purple
and all colors while making a difference in the world.
and don't just laugh, but laugh out loud,
and never miss out a chance to dance,
that, you will always regret.

you can't fight your destiny
but you can hug it and make it beautiful

acceptance/ grace/ creation

when you find yourself

the path looking back will not have the stories of losses
but that of the arrows that led you to you

the final understanding

dear princess warriors

education and wisdom,
skills and empowerment

don't protect you against pain
they don't predict a woundless war
they don't protect you from death either

dear one,

it makes you a well-armed
and well-trained warrior in the war of the world

it gives you a platform to know
what to stand for, how to stand for,
and how to make a difference

you may likely get more wounded
you may get a million times
more pain than those without,

but the thing is, whether
it's yours or someone else's pain

when you don't know what to do with pain,
it causes suffering
when you know what to do with pain,
it becomes a blessing

...

education and wisdom,
skills and empowerment,
give you tools to do just that,

how to turn pain into a blessing

if not for you, then for someone else
without them,
you are a princess in the battlefield
with only a tiara and dress,
needing approval and validation for her own existence

with them,

you are a queen with arrow and bow,
and a roaring heart, raging army,
and unabashed, unapologetic purpose in life

so, empower yourself,

learn, unlearn, and keep growing
the battlefield will keep changing
but you will get to write
your own complete fairytale
you will get to be
your own complete fairytale

other people's understanding
of your growth

is not your responsibility

your responsibility is to grow,
whether you are understood or not

be busy building
and learning yourself

what holds you back
does not exist

you cannot break me, i am already broken

and i am busy
making

beautiful
constellations

with
my fragments

my rock bottom has more life,
than your heavily marketed smooth surface

they said, your words have power
i said, my words have truth and truth is power

truth is how the inside of you breathes outside

getting off balance

i am usually asked how i balance it all.
ok so the answer is - i do not, i do not balance it all.
i don't balance it all and i don't have it all.

what if less was more?

...

i have very few needs that require deadlines
like paying taxes and making sure i go to work
and be useful, making sure i am doing something
good for myself and something good for someone else
and love the people that i love and be exactly who i am
and continue to grow.

i have dreams but they don't have me

i do let my life take over my body and health at times
and i allow it, i call it my mommy weight
when i gain weight writing books and creating art.
for each situation of my life
i allow me grace including pain and joy.

for me the only constant is change
and the only permanent fact is that
everything and everyone is temporary

i cannot function unless i am authentic and true to myself
 and be in a space of mind where whatever i do impacts
at least one person other than myself positively
via my writing, practicing medicine, or being in relationship
or creating art.

i don't want to have it all and i am not a list.

one day i played for a few minutes with someone
who was playing basketball alone, we had a blast...

i did it on my heels and so imperfectly and so joyfully.
so that's how i treat life like a basketball court,
join someone if you can, celebrating, experiencing,
helping and making someone smile on the way.

...

you don't even need to know everything,
but you should try to know as much as of yourself.

and remember no knowledge is worth anything
without love.

love as in

lover of all things and all beings,
lover of people,
lover of compassion,
lover of kindness,
lover of being temporary,
lover of growth,
lover of learning,
lover of forgiveness

i wish everyone a great physical, emotional and
spiritual health so they can be harvest life
out of living for the short time they are here.

cheers, to not having it all,
for being ok with not having it all
for even being ok with wanting it all

but making sure before you want something –
you are willing to spend yourself for that

be gentle with yourself and have fun.
and take things sincerely but not too seriously,

because this all ends one day.

choosing who we are

we have no control, absolutely no control
of where we are at times,
but we will always have a choice of who we are

we can transition from victim to victor
we can right the wrong,
we can take all of the pain and make a teacher out of it

we can turn into the sun in the stormiest of rains
and make our own rainbow that we deserve

we can turn each tragedy into an opportunity
to birth better version of ourselves

we can choose to support all women
despite being alone in our journey,

we can choose to be a princess,
a mother, a warrior, a queen,
a lover, a leader or whatever
each cell of our existence created us for.

and we can choose to dance when things fall apart
we can choose to make jazz
out of the chaos that life will be at times

yes, we can choose to be who we are
no matter where we are

i was born to tell you
your hands will always carry healing,
always,

so be brave and indulge
in this adventure called life

your breaking will be painful
but your healing will be glorious,
and godly,

that's the only way you will face
the highest version of the self,
the cosmos within

dr nivedita lakhera is a stroke survivor, divorce survivor,
heart break survivor and an assault survivor.
she is a poet & artist by soul.
she heals body via the practice of medicine and the soul
with the balm of words and art.

she was born and raised in new delhi, india. growing up in a
very loving and supportive family she walked with fairy tales
in her feet. but her otherwise beautiful life was jolted
and derailed by a stroke at the young age of 27, a divorce,
and then a heart break.
she turned to words and colors to rescue her soul.
and oh yes, they did rescue her. and now she wants to share
them with everyone. pillow of dreams was her first poetry book.

she sincerely believes beyond realms of time, classes, opinions,
births, and religion that all of us are connected by common
threads of love, losses, joys, sorrows, betrayal, support,
and friendship. and so, a poem, a verse, a phrase
becomes a temple where anyone and everyone
can visit and submit their soul to rest for a little bit
before embarking on the next journey,
before the next destination,
before the next turn, a retreat and oasis
of belonging and familiarity...
that all hearts beat the same!

just like life, there is no particular order in this book
but i hope something in this book holds you,
hugs you & celebrates you.

at times life will not make sense, that time come
and pick up this book.
at times life will make sense, that time, come
and pick up this book.

so, we can be together in both certain and uncertain times
with a comfort, the comfort that none of us is alone,
the comfort that destiny deliberately puts us where
at times endings and beginnings blur into each other
just like jazz in air.
so, come and let suffering dissolve in these pages and
let words become your legs when you are too weak to walk
come and let art be the interface where we all meet and greet
each other with no barrier of time, come and let us borrow
each other's strength and share what is ours, come and let us
pick at least one person in our life.

and at times that one person will need to be only you,
and i want you to know at that is not only enough
but it is marvelous and celebratory in every capacity.
there may be a timeline to this thing called life but
there is no timeline for loving, caring, learning and sharing
and that is what this book is all about.
again, this book was written with a lot of heart,
so please find extra love and forgiveness towards this
sincere but an imperfect attempt to reach out to you.
being soft, being real and being authentic allows me
to be vulnerable on these pages with the greatest strength
in the hope that someone somewhere can do the same
for themselves, because that is where healing begins.

so be kind to yourself no matter where you are and who you are.
much love and hugs for being with me till the end.
thanks for being here and thank you for being you.

Made in United States
North Haven, CT
13 November 2021

11123040R00116